Internet Marketing Secrets

All techniques for Online Marketing revealed

James Deboro

Copyright © 2012 James Deboro

All rights reserved.

ISBN: 9798615553639

CONTENTS

Introduction

Chapter One: The Benefits of Marketing Online............................	1
Chapter Two: Reaching Your Target Audience...............................	3
Chapter Three: Create Content that is Effective............................	7
Chapter Four: Generating Advertising that is Free.........................	13
Chapter Five: E-mail Marketing...	17
Chapter Six: Build a Community Online.......................................	23
Chapter Seven: Strategies for Co-Branding..................................	26
Chapter Eight: Rising to the Top of Search Engines........................	29
Chapter Nine: Building E-mail Lists..	35
Chapter Ten: Forgetting about SEO..	38
Chapter Eleven: Website Development..	42
Conclusion..	46

INTRODUCTION

If you have a business, and want online marketing results that are successful, you need to be a creative thinker and think outside of the box. The Internet is the perfect place for small businesses to establish their marketing campaign. Using the Internet for advertising is extremely cost-effective because it is so measurable and targeted towards the people you want to reach. Internet marketing allows you to compete with the competition and come out ahead.

This book will show you what you need to do to turn your online website into a resource that your customers can trust. You'll also learn how to get more customers to visit your website. The main goal of this book is to teach you which online marketing techniques are the most effective for your business. Some of the things that you'll learn include:

- How to design your website to that you attract the customers you want.
- How to reach your customers through e-mail marketing.
- Why co-branding is important.
- How to choose online partners that are right for you.
- How to create customized content for you website so that your customers visit frequently.
- How to establish yourself as an expert in your specific industry.
- How to use your marketing budget without overspending.

This book will give you the latest information in marketing trends so that you make the most of your marketing budget.

CHAPTER ONE: THE BENEFITS OF MARKETING ONLINE

Marketing rules are the same no matter how big or small your business is: (1) brand your product, (2) determine who your target audience is, (3) get the sales, and (4) establish repeat customers. Online marketing is very effective in managing all four of these rules.

Online Marketing Defined

The definition of online marketing is: Placing your business or product on the Internet for millions of users to access so that you can turn your website into a strong tool to maximize your sales and business potential.

But online marketing is much more than putting your advertising online. Marketing online includes such areas as communicating with your customers, promoting your business or product online, and making sure that your website content is useful and up to date. The great thing about online marketing is that you don't need to have a huge budget to put together a marketing campaign that is effective. There are tools that you can use to make your marketing techniques easy and profitable such website templates, shopping cart templates, and online marketing templates.

What You Need for Online Marketing to be Successful

There are some important points to consider before you get into the strategies and intricacies of online marketing:

- Communication. An important part of online marketing is how you respond to your customer's e-mail. You don't want to lose potential customers after you've made the effort to have them visit your website and then contact you for more information. E-mail is a very effective and cost efficient way for you to generate more sales. The key to this effectiveness is "consistency". You need to be consistent in your response to your customers. You'll also want to make sure that the tone of your e-mail corresponds with the tone you've set in your website content.

- Human Resources. If you're going to succeed online you need to have enough people working with you. Efficient websites incorporate a personal touch with a fast response time to customers. Your goal is to turn the visitors to your website into customers. The standard time for a return e-mail is from 48 to 72 hours. If you wait any longer to e-mail back you risk losing the customer. This means that if you don't have the man power to return e-mail in two to three days you need to take another look at your marketing strategy.
- Products people want to buy online. Before you start marketing online you need to be sure that you have a product or service that people want to buy. Customers need to find a value in what you're selling. There are two motivating factors when it comes to selling online: cost and convenience. Ask yourself if customers will find it easier to buy online than finding a local store. Is it cheaper for them to buy this from you online?

Online Goals

Once you've established that there is a need for your service or product you'll be ready to determine your business goal and whether or not you can meet this goal online. If your main goal is to sell a product online you should decide how you want to make those sales. For example, do you want customers to buy from you online or do you want them to come to you to close the sale? You'll need to decide what action is needed for the sale to be finalized. Small businesses need marketing efforts that are targeted and precise.

CHAPTER TWO: REACHING YOUR TARGET AUDIENCE

A big factor to successful online marketing is knowing who your target audience is and how to reach them. To determine what types of customers you are trying to reach you should be asking yourself the following questions:

- What age group are you trying to sell to?
- Are you selling to a specific ethnic group or gender?
- Will most of your customers be married or single?
- How fast will most Internet connections be?
- Will you target customers who have children?
- What level of education will most of your customers have?
- Where will most of your customers live?
- Will your customers have any specific hobbies?

The more you know about your customers the easier it will be to come up with a marketing plan. You'll also be able to design a website that is the most appealing to these customers. The biggest advantage of marketing on the Internet is that it allows you to become very targeted towards your desired customers.

Targeting Different Types of Customers

Marketing online is the same as marketing anywhere else. There are certain products, colors, themes, and lingo that will appeal more to some customers than to others. When you know what type of customers you're targeting you can meet their needs so that you grab their attention. When you use certain features that pull customers to your website you have the ability to gain their attention, loyalty, and trust. For example, studies show that most female shoppers like to save money and time. Over 80% of purchases in the home are influenced in some way by women. As well, these same studies show that women like to able to compare costs fast and easily without getting any kind of sales pressure. If you're trying to target women customers some things that you should keep in mind include (1) giving them a feeling of comfort and community, (2) let your website deal with everyday problems, and (3) focus on education, health, and family.

Get the Word Out

Doing something innovative and creative online, as well as using the latest technology, will always get attention. For example, adding animation, flash, or a photo can create a buzz about the product or service that you're selling. Just as e-mail, which contains jokes and strange pictures, gets forwarded all around the planet so too can your marketing message make the rounds. Come up with a marketing message and then forward it to family, friends, and anyone else you know.

Any time that you can get someone else to forward your e-mail to others you get the information out there about your website and the product or service you're selling. One key to great online marketing is remembering that quality, not quantity, counts. Avoid buying e-mail lists and focus instead on building your own with people who are actually interested in what you're selling. Today online marketing isn't about how many people you get to your website or how many people are on your e-mail list. Today online marketing is all about how people react to your website and what it is that you're selling.

Personalizing Your Website

Even if you're not selling a product or service that is for a specific target audience you need to have a website that is personalized. For example, even though Amazon sells products that appeal to all target audiences they have still managed to create a personalized website that fits every customer. This is the goal of personalization technology.

Try to limit the number of products or services that you're offering to your customers. "Information overload" is one of the biggest problems on the Internet. If you give your customers too many choices they'll have a hard time making a decision. The key to avoiding information overload is organization as well as making sure that products and services are directed towards your customers.

Don't make the mistake of thinking that online marketing stop when you generate a sale. Your current customers are the ideal way for you to reach new customers. You want to get leads from your customers by using marketing concepts such as "tell a friend" e-mails.

One mistake that many small online businesses make is to focus only on self-promotion. The bottom line is that customers don't care about you. They only care about what it is that you're selling and what you can do for them. When someone visits your website you have about ten seconds to get their attention before they move on to the next website. That means that you have ten seconds to tell this person why it is that they need you. The home page of your website should tell people why your service or product is just right for them. Your home page should include information about your company and/or have a personal bio about who you are.

If you're not sure about whether your website is reaching the right people, ask them. If you provide something of value to people who visit your website they'll give you information. Things of value include contests, coupons, and free products. Make sure that you let them know they can trust you by including a privacy policy on your website that states you won't share any personal information they provide with anyone else. Stick to your policy and never sell the information your customers provide you with. Otherwise you'll lose and abuse their trust.

Once you know the demographics of your customers you'll know how to spend your marketing budget. You can focus your online promotions using targeted marketing strategy. Even though you may end up with fewer people visiting your website, targeted online marketing is the way to go.

Using Banner Ads

One mistake that many online businesses make is using banner ads to reach the greatest amount of people. Your focus when it comes to banner ads is to reach the right type of people for the product or service that you're selling. One thing to keep in mind is that, if you have a limited budget, you should avoid buying banner ads altogether. If you have a big budget, banner ads can be great for branding your company. You'll be able to negotiate contracts that are long term with affiliated websites in your area of business. However, the results of click-through marketing are usually low and this makes banner ads the least cost effective of all online marketing techniques.

If you decide that you want to purchase banner ads you should focus on buying them on web pages that are very targeted. Ads are cheaper the more targeted a web page is. And the cheaper the ad the more cost effective your banner ads will be.

Another way that you can target the placement of your banner ads is to embed them in web page content. Before you purchase a banner ad find out what content the website administrators will be including on their web page that may be related to your online business. If the website uses a keyword search tool ask that your banner ads appear when key words that are linked to your product or service are typed into the search engine by visitors to the website.

Try to place your banner ads on a web page that is as deep into the website as possible. This way you'll be reaching people who are truly looking for information that relates to your business. This is a great strategy to use if you want to get the most value for your online budget. Again, if your budget for marketing is quite high, you'll want to buy banner ads on the home pages of websites so that your brand reaches a lot of people.

Keywords

One of the most cost effective ways to use your online marketing budget is to buy keywords. You can find out the price of keywords that are specific to your industry at www.Overture.com. You want your keywords to be as targeted and specific as possible. Always remember the goal of your business and buy keywords that encourage people to visit your website. Keywords that are general will cost you more and at the same time will attract fewer customers to your website. Before you start buying keywords you need to look at the content of your website. You want to buy keywords that are effective for your business content and that keep people coming back to your website.

CHAPTER THREE: CREATE CONTENT THAT IS EFFECTIVE

The Internet is designed to be changing and dynamic. People who visit your website want to see content that is new and filled with ideas and business promotions. If people visit your website and don't see new content on a frequent basis they'll think that your site is stagnant and has been abandoned without any customer service there for them to rely on. The home page of your website is one of the most important aspects of your online marketing strategy. It's the content of your home page that gives your business a brand. The more useful and professional the information on your home page is the more credit you bring to your product or service.

The Internet is one of the best places for consumers to find out about new products and services. This places the net above television, radio, magazines, and newspapers. When you use the Internet to promote your product or service you have the opportunity to reach a multitude of potential customers anywhere at any time. The web is one of the most powerful mediums for reaching and influencing people and the decisions they make about business.

Components of Good Content

One of the key ingredients to success on the Internet is creating website content that Internet users want to read. When you have content that is (1) interesting, (2) factual, and (3) well written, you have some of the main tools that you need to get the desired traffic to your online website.

Writing Decisions: When you first start writing content for your website you'll find yourself facing many decisions before you even sit down at the keyboard or pick up a pen. As you begin to develop the content on your website pages you'll find that you're often changing many of your first instinct decisions. This is all part of the process of writing. But how can you most efficiently sort out all you need to think about so that you develop website content that users want to read?

It's important that you find out what it is that Internet users are looking for on the Internet so that you can focus your website content on these issues. Take some time to study at the top hits in the search engines for products or services that are similar to what you're selling. Even though these top ranked websites are most likely using Search Engine Optimization techniques you can still read what it is that they're using to draw in the crowd. Take some of these concepts and include them in the flow of your web content....but ONLY if these concepts enhance what you're writing and are entirely relevant to the products or services that you're selling. Keep in mind that although one website may be at the top of the search engine rankings today, it won't take them long to fall back into the ranks of "mediocre websites". Websites that rely on SEO techniques don't give people the information that they're looking for to keep them coming back. How many times have you yourself searched a topic in a search engine only to find that the top hit is filled with articles and web content that has nothing to do with what the website is all about?

People who use the Internet are looking for one or more of the following components:

- Entertainment
- Information
- Community issues

If your website provides at least one of these components you're on your way to attracting potential customers and repeat customers. Websites that contain valuable content not only bring credit to your business but also position your company as an expert in your business industry. Keeping your website fresh with new content doesn't have to be an overwhelming task. There are cost-efficient and time-saving techniques you can take advantage of to keep your website up to date at all times…without having to hire hundreds of people to help you!

Dynamic Home Page: One way that you can have an ever changing home page is to design five to ten unique pages and then rotate them every month. Take a couple of weeks to design different ideas for your home page. Create random page promotions that include a message that is timeless or that have seasonal images with announcements such as "Holiday Specials". When you design different features for you home page all at one time you're forced to look at your marketing strategy for at least one year. This will save you a lot of time since you then won't have to think about your home page content for about 12 months. A web developer can put your home pages on a rotating script or use an automatic timer. You can then rotate your home pages to highlight a new tip every month or to promote a featured product. The home page of your website is much like the front cover of a magazine. People want to see a home page that has different photos and content at least every month. You won't want all of the content of your website to be featured on the home page as this will overwhelm your website visitors. Choosing one or two features to highlight each month is much more effective. The rest of your website content should be well organized within the rest of the pages of your site. When you're ready to update your home page all you have to do is grab content from other web pages. This way you're not always having to create new content but are reorganizing your current content so that people think it's new.

Changing your Home Page Too Often: Even though you want your website to be new and dynamic you also don't want to change it too often. People who surf the Internet take comfort from their favorite websites and want them to be familiar. If you change your home page too often you may confuse people who come to your website on a frequent basis. You also run the risk of compromising your positioning in search engines if you don't maintain some type of consistency on your home page. When you're updating the content on your home page you want to make sure that you don't confuse people. When you make changes to graphics or content it shouldn't change the way your website looks and feels. Regular visitors to your website should be able to find the same information that they've always found on your home page. In short, the headers and navigation tools on your home page shouldn't ever change. Change content and images with other content and images while maintaining the sites original functionality. Home pages that are consistent lend a feeling of comfort to users. If your customers learn to expect consistency they'll also learn to rely on your quality customer service. If you're a small online business, gaining your customer's trust is synonymous to dependability.

Search Engine Positioning: Search engine positioning can be affected by the changes you make to your home page. There are some search engines that "spider" websites anywhere from three weeks to three months. These search engines take a look at all aspects of your website from the home page content to the tags you have for your graphics. Your website will be ranked higher the longer your keywords remain consistent. You need to find a balance between keeping things on your home page new and exciting while at the same time keeping things familiar and similar. The best way for you to achieve this is to keep most of your home page the way it is and change only a portion of it. This allows visitors to your website to see new content and you won't have to worry about your website disappearing from search engine rankings.

Benefits of a Flexible Home Page: Once you've mastered the technique of updating your home page, while at the same time keeping the core content the same, you'll be well on your way to recognizing the benefits of a flexible home page. A flexible home page lets you test your offline marketing efforts. Before you spend money on a magazine or newspaper ad you can test it out on your website. You'll be able to see how people react to the ad. Your home page will let you determine which featured products attract the most interest. You can also determine which graphics generate the most attraction. You'll need web tracking software to get this type of information. Tracking software lets you obtain marketing data that is detailed and precise. You'll be able to see which graphics people have clicked on as well as what web page they were on just before they left your website.

Content if You Don't Write: If you don't write, or know how to take photographs, there are still some things that you can do to generate content for your website:

- Buy content: You can buy images and photographs that are of high quality without spending a lot of money. Spending a few hundred dollars on some great images will go a long way in giving your website a professional look. There are many websites on the Internet where you can find images and photographs that relate to your business. It's not recommended that you buy written content for the simple reason that it's not cost effective. Many of the services on the Internet that supply written content are geared towards large online companies that have a big marketing budget. The goal of content on your website is to make your company and product appear credible. You can accomplish this by having a few well placed articles on your web pages.
- Let customers create content: You can have your customers generate content for your website. One way to do this is by creating a section entitled "Frequently Asked Questions". Here your customers can ask you questions about your product or service and you can list your answers. You can rotate this type of information and feature a different question every week. Another way to create content is by holding a contest by asking customers to send you

stories about how they enjoy your product or how it has helped them in some way. You can offer a special prize such as a coupon for free product. You can take the best written stories and post them on your web pages. Not only is this type of material great content for your website, it also acts as a testimonial.
- Links to other content: Another way that you can get updated content for your website without having to write it yourself is by posting headlines of related news items to your website. Then simply provide a link from the headline to the original article. Content for small businesses on the Internet doesn't have to be original. It should, however, be useful to the people who are reading your website. The content you choose for your website will show your customers that you care enough about the information that you're providing them with to post links to original articles. This information can include anything from health issues to new items to information about family. Make sure that you accurately quote your sources and never copy articles without first getting permission.

The Importance of Communication: One thing that you need to remember as you make the decisions about what you want to say on your website is the importance of communication in anything that you write. These days competition for communication on the Internet is difficult. The sheer volume of information being routed on the Internet is a huge communications barrier. Every day people on the web are bombarded with websites and businesses lobbying for their attention.

People are busy and time is short. So it's all the more important to know how to get your marketing message across. The key aspects of good customer communication inclue:

- the ability to read customers
- the ability to understand which communication style your customers are most likely to pay attention to, and
- the ability to adapt your website content for your customers.

When you communicate with your customers through the Internet you have only one shot at communicating your marketing message. You need to keep in mind that those customers, and potential customers, reading your marketing message don't have a long time to read what you have to say....so you better say it fast, accurately, and in words that they want to hear. Learn how to keep it simple and direct.

There are some basic ideas that you should keep in mind when you're writing website content that customers want to read:

- Identify and clarify the marketing message that you want to get across to your customers. When you pinpoint your focus you have the ability to zoom in and give your customers content that they can rely on and trust.
- Gather information. Don't just write website content for the sake of filling up your web space. Find out what customers want to read and then write for them
- Evaluate the information that you're writing about. Make sure that the information that you're basing your website content on is precise and reliable. Does the information represent the points of view about your online business that you want to get across? Is the information fact or opinion? Many times a combination of (1) fact, and (2) customer opinion, go hand in hand for writing web content that people want to read.
- Consider the alternatives and implications of what you write. Make sure that you draw the appropriate conclusions from what you write and that your readers will draw the same conclusions about your web content. What are the costs, benefits, and consequences of the content that you have on your website? Take the time to weigh the advantages and disadvantages of moving away from Search Engine Optimization techniques and instead focusing on writing what people want to read.

CHAPTER FOUR: GENERATING ADVERTISING THAT IS FREE

One of the best ways to get leads on the Internet is by getting a product mention or a free link on another website. Effective online marketing is all about putting your product or service in front of potential customers at the exact time that they are looking for it. This technique is known as "pinpoint marketing". Pinpoint marketing is much different than advertising on radio or television, which are known as "interruptive marketing" techniques. Interruptive marketing costs a lot more than pinpoint marketing and is less effective for the simple reason that you're attempting to put your product out there in front of everybody instead of pinpointing those potential customers who want to find out more about you and your business.

Pinpoint Marketing: Pinpoint marketing is the process of sending the right message at the right time so that it produces actual results. For example, if you're at a ball game and are eating a bag of popcorn. Just when you take a handful of popcorn the Coca-Cola logo appears on the big screen. The next you thing you know you're looking for the first vendor who can sell you a can of Coke. However, if an advertisement for a new car appears on the big screen while you're watching the game and eating popcorn, you're less likely to be interested since it's not something you're looking for at that moment. Interruptive marketing isn't really targeted because it's not something that you are actively looking for. People who use the Internet are usually looking for a solution to a problem. When you put your product in front of them at the right time you've reached a potential customer.

Day-part Marketing: The placement and timing of ads on the Internet has become so important to online marketing that some companies, such as Yahoo!, are selling advertisements in "day-part". Day-part is something that has always been done in television advertising. Day-part marketing works like this – specifying at which time of the day certain ads are viewed so that you can effectively target your customers.

Embedded Marketing Messages: These days, more people than ever are using the Internet to research a product before they buy. As well, most Internet users are becoming more serious about the amount of time that they spend online. Studies show that users are spending less time on the web and that the time they do spend surfing is focused and deliberate. Many users bookmark their favorite websites so that they can access information fast and easily. When people want a solution to a certain problem, such as a health issue or taking a vacation, they often look online for the answers. This is why it's important for you to put your product or service right in front of them whenever you can.

Establish Credibility

One of the main problems with online marketing is establishing credibility with your customers. Since there are so many Internet scams out there people are wary of whom they do business with and even more cautious of companies they are unfamiliar with. As a small business you need to gain credibility on the Internet by making your logo and company name a familiar item to Internet users. One way that you can achieve this credibility is by setting up a shopping cart on Yahoo! You'll not only have access to the technology of shopping carts you'll also find yourself affiliated with a familiar and successful online company. This gives customers the confidence needed to do business with you. When a customer buys something from your online Yahoo! Store they become more familiar with the name of your company and will be more likely to buy from you directly at your website the next time around.

Get your Content to Other Websites: Another way that you can build credibility online is to swap content. If you can position an article that includes a link to your website on another website that is at the top of the field of your industry you increase your chances of credibility. This then increases your sales potential. But just how do you get web editors to take any notice of your company? In chapter 3 you learned the value of web content for companies of all sizes. You also learned how expensive it can be to purchase web content. The bottom line is that more companies are willing to trade a free mention on your website for a good article. This way the content provider gets targeted and free advertising for their product or service, and the company that is posting the article (and the link) can feature content that is informative and valuable.

You can get some great leads by writing articles. When a potential customer reads your article you establish yourself as an expert in your field. When the customer links over to your website you have a very good lead that can generate sales.

People who use the Internet want results that are immediate. They know exactly what they are looking for so your advertising message needs to be appropriate, concise, and to the point. You need to think about what kind of people will be accessing the website where you plan to post your article.

Swapping Advertising: A great way to get your product information out to people is by using links, banner ads, coupons, and swapping articles. If you're in the home renovation business you can trade articles with other businesses such as painters and electricians. In fact, you can trade articles with anyone in your chosen industry that isn't in direct competition with you. Extra content on your website will give you more credibility while having your articles on other websites will lend your company a position of authority.

Word of Mouth Marketing

The second most common way that people find new websites is word of mouth. Search engines are the number one way. Word of mouth can be generated from message board postings by virtual strangers or by e-mailing friends. Effective word of mouth is known as "viral marketing" and is one of the biggest success stories on the Internet.

Viral marketing works in much the same way urban legends and funny jokes on the Internet work as they are forwarded all around the world. Viral marketing takes advantage of the socialization needs of society. No matter how small the social network starts out as, effective viral marketing can turn a small unknown company into one that is known everywhere in the online world. Some of the biggest companies on the Internet rely on viral marketing to stay successful. You can set up an effective e-mail marketing strategy without a big budget or a lot of technology. All you need to do is set up an e-mail signature that has a marketing message within it. This marketing message will be attached to any e-mail that your company sends. Messages are easily set up through Outlook and other e-mail programs.

You can take the concept of e-mail messages one step further by attaching your marketing message to all mail that is outgoing. This is done through a simple process known as "mail rerouting". When you use this process you can track the results as well as know for sure that every outgoing message will look and feel the same no matter whether you or your employees send the mail.

Something for Free: Everyone wants to get something that is free. When you offer something that is free the word will spread very quickly. And free offers will bring traffic to your website. However, most small online businesses can't afford to give away much for free. What you can do is become creative and offer a free product for the first 20 people who buy another product from your website. This can be as simple as movie tickets.

Message Boards and Chatrooms: Message boards and chatrooms are great places for word of mouth and viral marketing to flourish. This is particularly true for those people who are 25 years of age and younger. In chatrooms people share ideas and concepts and this can lead to some great leads for your business.

E-mail makes it easy for people to share ideas and concepts with others anywhere in the world. If you can attach your marketing message to these infectious e-mails you'll be able to create a buzz and stir about your product or service. When potential customers recognize your logo or company name you're on your way to gaining trust, credibility, and the close of a sale.

Domain Names: One last thing to remember when you're trying to spread information about your company is the effectiveness of a memorable domain name. You want to pick a domain name that is easy to remember, easy to spell, and that relates to what you're selling. When people easily find your website you'll want to make sure that your home page content is dynamic so they keep returning.

CHAPTER FIVE: E-MAIL MARKETING

As the Internet has grown, e-mail marketing has become one of the most efficient and cost effective tools for online marketing. E-mail marketing drastically affects businesses whether they are B2B or B2C (business to business/business to consumer). Marketing through e-mail increases your brand loyalty and increases your customer service through the eyes of your customers. When permission based e-mail marketing is done right it can be more effective than any other type of online marketing strategy. The thing to keep in mind is that no one single component of online marketing can stand on its own. For instance, an e-mail newsletter needs to have a great website to back it up as well as interest in your business to build your e-mail list in the first place.

The number one activity online is e-mail. This is why e-mail can be used as a great online marketing tool. Many Internet users say that they would rather get marketing messages in their e-mail than be bothered by sales phone calls at home.

Permission Based E-mail

One important key to an effective e-mail marketing strategy is to only focus on permission based mail. This means that customers need to choose to receive mail from you. This is known as "opt in".

You should never rent or buy an e-mail list since this is considered to be spam. No matter what the owner of the e-mail list will tell you, the majority of the addresses on the list did not opt in to receive e-mail or to have their personal information sold to you. When you send e-mail to people who don't want it you're sending spam. Spam will give your company image a cheap look and take away any trust that customers have in you. You want leads that are quality and not quantity and this means building your own e-mail list. You'll find that the final results will be tremendous to you and your business.

E-mail marketing should be considered an extension of the customer service that you provide. You want to be able to communicate with your customers at every point in the sales process. When you give your customers what they ask for, without abusing any permission, you establish the base for a relationship that is founded on respect and leads to long term customer loyalty.

Build your E-mail List

It takes time to build an e-mail list but once you do you'll have the names of people who are genuinely interested in what you're selling. The one thing you need to remember is not to abuse a person's trust once they give you their private information and e-mail address. Let your customers know that you value their trust and will respect their privacy. You can do this through a privacy policy on your website where you promise not to sell information to other businesses or vendors. You can go so far as to let your customers know what you'll be e-mailing them and how often they can expect it. Always provide people with the option to remove themselves from your e-mail list. This promotes customer confidence.

If you take part in joint promotion and/or co-branding with another online company make sure that you don't trade e-mail lists. What you can do is include information about that company in the newsletter you send to your customers. All e-mail should come only from you. You'll lose your customer's trust if they think you've sold their personal information to another business. And this means that they will disregard any future communication with you and your business.

To get people to join your e-mail list don't ask them for much more than a few bits of information at a time. You need to gain their trust before asking for too much information. You can start out by asking for their name and e-mail address. Your future marketing promotions will help you fill in other information such as age and demographics. It will take time to get a clear idea of who your best customers are and what they want to get out of your website and e-mail newsletter.

If customers have trust in your business it won't be hard to get an e-mail list together. Gaining trust is as easy as holding a contest, offering discounts or coupons, regularly changing your website content, or providing informative newsletters.

Should you have on offline store, a great way to gather e-mail addresses is by asking people to give you their business card if they want to win a free lunch. Other offline methods of gathering e-mail addresses include networking events and trade shows. A good rule of thumb is: if someone gives you their business card that has their e-mail address on it you can safely assume that it's okay to send them an e-mail at least once. If they don't respond back you should then assume that they are not interested. Take these non-respondents off your e-mail list.

Goal Oriented Marketing: After you've created your e-mail list it's time to develop an e-mail marketing plan. Determine what your business goal is and how you plan to achieve this goal: through (1) repeat customers? (2) more leads? (3) e-mail marketing? You want to define your goals as well as you can so that you can keep track of the process.

E-mail Newsletters

If you're going to send a newsletter via e-mail you need to provide incentives for people to want to stay on your e-mail list.

Ideas for Content: You don't always have to offer discounts or a free product as incentives to customers. The content of your newsletter can also be a good incentive. Good newsletter content includes:

- Customer submitted success stories.
- Information from experts in your industry.
- A section for questions and answers.
- News and/or statistics about your industry.
- Feedback from customers.
- Tips about your products or services.

Your newsletter shouldn't include information such as "about you", your company history, or your company news. This type of information is only valuable for investors. The bottom line is that your customers don't really care about what is happening in your business. They only want to know what you can do for them. Good newsletter content is anything that catches the interest of your customers. A newsletter, just like your home page, has only a few seconds to attract the attention of your customer before they decide to delete it. Your newsletter should immediately let your customer know what you can do for them, how you're going to do it, and why they should do business with you. Newsletters are a great way to promote your business but make sure that you take into consideration the content, the length, and the frequency of the newsletter.

Keep it Short: Your newsletter should be concise, short, and get to the point. It should be no more than 1000 words and deal with no more than five different products or services at one time. People don't like to read lengthy e-mails.

Newsletters that deal with too many departments are more difficult for you to update. This could be a roadblock to you sending out newsletters on a regular basis while at the same time providing new and fresh content. If there is too much information in the first e-mail your customers won't want to click through to your website. And a no-click means you have no way to keep track of the success or failure of your e-mail marketing strategy.

The main difference between online marketing and traditional marketing is that online methods allow you to track what is happening. If the e-mails you send out don't encourage customers to click to your website you won't know what is working and what isn't.

Frequency and Timing: You need to determine when and how often you're going to send out e-mail newsletters. You don't want to send e-mails out too often as this will overwhelm your customers. At the same time, you don't want to wait too long between e-mails or your customers will start to forget who you are. Timing and consistency will vary depending on what type of business you have. If you're not sure when and how often to send your newsletters, just ask. Whenever someone joins your e-mail list ask them how often they would like to receive an e-mail from you. Another way to track frequency and timing is by sending out e-mails at different times during the week. Then keep track of which days have more viewings of your e-mail and your website to determine what day is the better one for sending out your newsletter.

List Hosting Services

You can build, send, and keep track of your e-mail marketing campaign by using an e-mail hosting program. Using an e-mail program is an important method of effective online marketing. An e-mail hosting service takes away some of the work of manually adding and deleting addresses from your database. These services also have the ability to test your newsletters before you send them out. There are multiple templates for you to choose from which means that you won't have to learn how to use html in order to send a newsletter that is professional looking. If you decide to use a template make sure that it matches the look and feel of your company brand and website. Consistency is the key to effective online marketing.

E-mail list hosting services allow you to track and manage your e-mail marketing campaign. You have the ability to receive reports that have precise details about which links and graphics your customers have clicked on. This information lets you change the content of your newsletter when you know what it is that your customers most want to read and see. As you start to send out more newsletters you'll get a better feel for what it is that your customers want. This is why you want the content of your newsletters to be flexible.

You should create newsletter content that is somewhat based on the profiles of the customers you're trying to reach. The majority of e-mail list services will allow you to set up your subscription pages so that your customers can indicate what they want to receive from your company. When you can identify the audience that you're writing for you can modify your newsletter so that you include the right kinds of promotions and product information.

If your newsletter contains something of value, such as travel information, your customers are more likely to forward the e-mail on to friends and family. When you establish yourself as an expert in your industry, by giving your customers the information they want to see, you build credibility and trust.

Always keep in mind that no matter how great your newsletter content is, there is no guarantee that people will read it. One way that you can make sure your newsletter isn't deleted before being read is by have a great subject line.

Great Subject Lines

Many newsletters and business offers are never read by Internet users for the simple reason that the e-mail didn't have an effective subject line. A subject line may only be a few words but these few words are very important.

As more and more e-mails fill our in-boxes it's more important than ever to have a subject line that catches our attention. The subject line is one of the most important aspects of your e-mail marketing campaign because it's what creates a first impression for your business. With just a few words you can encourage someone to read your newsletter or you can cause them to delete your e-mail without another glance.

Here are some simple rules for creating a great subject line:

- Keep the subject line direct and short. Subject lines should never be more than ten words long. In fact, five words or less is the perfect length. Most e-mail browsers won't let users see more than five or six words so a longer subject line will be truncated and not seen by the user. Use strong and descriptive words rather than fluffy adjectives such as "very".
- Emphasize the benefits to the reader. You want to make it as easy as possible for your customers to know precisely why they will benefit from reading your newsletter. This can be as simple as a "reward" for just opening the e-mail. A reward can be information or a discount coupon. You want to use catch phrases such as "save money" and "save time" to get a reader's immediate attention. The key is to entice your customers to want to read more and open the e-mail.
- Ask questions. When you ask a question in the subject line you cause a reader to become curious and want to know more. As well, when you ask a question the e-mail sounds more like it's coming from a colleague rather than just a business and will more likely be opened and read.
- Personal subject lines. One big mistake that screams "spam" is sending your e-mail to "undisclosed recipients". Make sure to always use your company name or real name as the sender. Try to put the recipients name in the subject line if there is room as well as insert it into the greeting of the e-mail.
- Take advantage of holidays and current events. If there is an upcoming holiday, such as Christmas, you can tie it up with your e-mail subject line. For example, "Save time on your Christmas Shopping".
- Avoid using the word "free". Hard sales phrases, such as "free" and "limited offer", are often filtered out by e-mail services since they are a clear indication of spam. As well, try to avoid using hype which includes explanation marks or all capital letters.

CHAPTER SIX: BUILD A COMMUNITY ONLINE

Over 93% of Internet users take part in some type of online community. But just why are online communities such a draw for so many people?

- Online communities are much like a virtual café, bar, or other gathering place for people to get together with people with similar interests.
- Online communities are a great place to learn something new.
- Online communities are where people can be anonymous and share their problems and fears.
- Online communities allow people to talk with people of the same mind so that they can confirm their beliefs.
- Online communities allow people who are facing a hardship to feel less lonely.

Online Community Defined: An online community can be accessed anywhere at any time. Some of the components of an online community include chatrooms, message boards, newsletters, event calendars, and anything else that lets an Internet user interact with others who are online.

Why should you be concerned about online communities for your online marketing strategy? Customers who take part in an online community are a good target for your sales because they have a high affinity for loyalty to your product when they are participating in an online community. When you have a strong and solid online customer community you know that you've built a loyal following for your company and the products or services you sell. Your loyal customers will spread news of your company through word of mouth and this will further increase your sales.

Message Boards: It will be to your benefit to provide your customers with a message board on your website. You can break your message board up into categories for your different products or services and encourage your customers to share their ideas and opinions with others. This is the first step towards building an online community. Customers will answer each others questions and this will save you some money on the cost of customer care. You just need to make sure that you moderate the message board on a regular basis so that your customers are getting accurate information.

Message boards also give you some great feedback about the products or services you're selling. Honest feedback from customers lets you better take care of their needs. You also get to learn a lot more about your customers and what it is that they want from your business.

Message boards are an important part of your website and your online community. You can develop a message board without spending a lot of time and money. Begin by asking your website hosting company if they can provide you with a message board template that you can include in the hosting package. Otherwise look on the Internet for a message board that is free. Choose a message board that fits the look and feel of your website so that you're maintaining consistency.

Message Board Content: A successful online community isn't just a common message board. The content on your website will play a big part in the quality of your online community. The more professional your website content is the better the quality of the message board. Always keep in mind that it's content that attracts readers and should be your major concern when it comes to your decision to develop an online community.

You'll find that fresh content ideas will start to flow when you have an online community. You'll know exactly what your customers are looking for and just how you can provide that for them. Active message boards are a cost efficient way for you to provide great customer service.

Message Board Calendar: Calendars are a vital part of the online community because they allow people to meet offline. Even if your company doesn't have any offline events, a calendar will let you post valuable industry information. For example, if your company sells stationary you could list the dates when you'll be attending trade fairs in the search for new products for your customers. This type of information lets customers know that your website and business content is ever changing.

Contests: Contests are a great way to get customers excited about your company and your website. Ask customers to share a story about how your product or service has benefited them. When the contest is over you can post these stories, along with the names of the winners, on your website. This marketing technique provides you with customer testimonials and is also a good way for you to see what your customers are interested in.

Maintaining an Online Community: It can take a lot of work to maintain your online community. You'll need to invest a certain amount of time and effort if you want the benefits of an online community to come your way. Make sure that all of your staff is involved in the maintenance of the community and that they know the importance of responding immediately to posts from your customers. When your online community is in its beginning stages you might have to plant some of your own questions, answers, and comments to the message board. Once traffic to your online community builds it will start to flow on its own and will require less maintenance.

Other Online Communities and Ad Space: If you don't think that you have the time and manpower to maintain an online community you might want to consider buying ad space on a community that is already established and which has a high profile on the Internet. The online community should have some connection with the types of products or services that you're selling.

CHAPTER SEVEN: STRATEGIES FOR CO-BRANDING

Online co-branding can be a little complicated. If an Internet user clicks on a link on your website and is taken to a web page that has a different brand or company it can get a bit confusing. They will wonder why they have been directed to an entirely different web page with unrelated content. When it comes to co-branding you need to choose partnerships that have something in common with the product or service that you're selling.

Co-branding can be very cost effective, particularly for small online businesses. However, if you choose the wrong partner, or too many partners, it might be more harmful than beneficial.

Adding Partners to your Website

As a small business you need to be cautious with your marketing budget. When you add a partner to your website you need to ensure that you're going to see strong and positive results from the union. These positive results can include more traffic to your website, increased online sales, or more contact with your customers. Online branding can be costly so be sure to choose partners that can benefit your business.

Co-branding is known by a variety of definitions that include:

- Joint promotions
- Value endorsements
- Joint ventures
- Alliances

Co-branding works best when both you and your partner company each provide a related service or product to the same types of customers.

Powerful Co-branding: Studies show that most online users like the idea of co-branding because it helps them to make decisions about the hundreds of brand name products that they come into contact with on the Internet. When top-quality brands join together in a partnership it strengthens their customer's approval. If you have a lesser know brand it will be to your benefit to partner up with a more well known brand so that your overall image is improved and so that you get more exposure on the Internet. And if a popular brand partners up with a lesser known brand it won't harm the popular brand. Your best bet is to partner up with a company that is equal to you.

A partnership needs to make sense and customers need to understand the connection.

Guidelines for Co-branding: If you have the right partner you can share the costs of marketing as well as strengthen your company brand. You'll also have access to a larger customer base. Following are some important co-branding guidelines:

- What does your co-brand partnership say to your customers? Will it make your customers feel better about themselves?
- What do you and your partner have in common? Are both of your products innovative? Are they dependable? You want to make sure that your image makes sense for your current customer base. You don't want to lose your current customer base but instead you want to build on it.
- How does your co-branding partnership benefit your customers? Will it save them money? Or will it save them time? Your marketing campaign should make the benefit very clear to your customers.
- Your goal with co-branding should be to find the best solutions for your customers.
- There should be an equal value for both brands in the partnership. You need to have an equal partnership or your marketing strategy will be uneven.
- Will your customers easily be able to see the connection and value of your partnership?
- Does the co-branding partnership bring you into contact with new customers?

The above guidelines need to be answered before you join in a co-branding partnership. Joint promotions take a great deal of time and thought to be implemented correctly. However, when done correctly and accurately, a co-branding partnership can bring you results that are far better than other traditional online marketing methods.

One of the basic rules of online marketing is: take your message, content, and promotions to your customers rather than focusing too much energy on the effort of trying to bring customers to your website.

Integrating Partnership Products

When it comes to co-branding partnerships you need to take the time to include the benefits of both brands into the overall design of your marketing promotions. This way your customers will understand the connection between both products or services.

Simply putting your company logo, or a link to your website, on another company's website will save you time and money but at the same time may cause you to lose some potential customers. Co-branding that is successful never leaves your customers wondering exactly what website they are on. Partnerships should improve a customer's shopping experience by helping them to make buying decisions. You'll want to exchange content with your partner so that you both expand your expertise in the industry. However, you'll need to incorporate this content into your website so that it flows naturally and fits in with your own content. The end result will be beneficial to both of you when you maintain professional consistency.

Complementary Partners: Your website will be more legitimate and competitive when you have co-branding content that is well integrated into your own web pages. Co-branding will only help your business if it complements the business goals you have defined for your company. Always keep your business goals in mind no matter what online marketing strategy you're trying to incorporate into your business. This means that all your website content, promotions, and activities with your co-branding partners encourages your customers to follow through with the sales action.

CHAPTER EIGHT: RISING TO THE TOP OF SEARCH ENGINES

The most common way for people to access your website is through search engines. And this means that whether you're selling a product or service, or just want to get some free press about your business, your company website needs to found by the top Internet search engines such as Google and Yahoo! Keeping up with search engines and their technology will be a full time job. However, if your website is well designed, search engines can be your best ally in generating more Internet traffic.

Search Engine Optimization Defined

Search engine optimization, or SEO, is the technique of placing your website so that its ranking increases in search engine databases. You want your website to have a high ranking and be as relevant as possible to a user's search.

Successful SEO websites use articles and keywords that are based on those words that Internet users type into search engines when they are looking for a particular product or service. As you're building your website you want to ensure effective keyword placement in all of the content and in the HTML coding of each web page.
When you submit your website to the most popular search engines you'll want to make sure that you're making the most of optimized keywords, as discussed in chapter 2. Your ranking in a search engine directory is closely connected to the quality of your website. If your chosen industry is in a competitive market you need to make sure that you have as many people as possible visit your website so that you get those sales and, in effect, make the most of your online marketing campaign.

The more you understand about how important targeted keywords are the better able you'll be to find the right marketing methods and solutions for your business.

Optimizing your Website

One of the most important things for you to remember when you're optimizing your website for search engines is that these engines read text and ignore graphics. This means that you need to focus on the text that is part of your website content.

The Right Keywords: Internet users will type keyword phrases into the search engine when they want to find a certain product or service. Most users will type about two or three words and then do a search for relevant websites. Before you spend a lot of time optimizing your website you should use a software program to help you determine which keyword phrases get the greatest search volume. This will allow you to focus your efforts on optimizing your website for the right keywords.

Text on your Home Page: Once you've decided which keywords are best for optimizing your website you'll want to put those keywords and phrases into the content of your website. You'll want to start by focusing on the first paragraph on your home page since this is the first thing that most search engines read to determine if your website is relevant to a user's search. In that first paragraph you'll want to use as many keywords and key phrases as you can so that your website comes up in a variety of user searches.

Using HTML Tags: You'll need to make sure that you have the right tags in your HTML coding so that it corresponds with the text on your website. Your ranking in search engines will be more solid if you're consistent with your tags and text.

Submitting Your Website to Search Engines

Registration with search engines, such as MSN, Yahoo, and Google, is crucial if you want to attract people to your website. Before you decide what search engines to submit to, you should do a careful study of what features each engine provides. Some of the features that you should be focused on include (1) how they promote websites, (2) what they offer in regards to advertising, and (3) if they have any other resources available. There are analyzers available on the Internet that will help you compare search engines. Your online marketing budget should include money and time so that you can find the right search engine for your business.

There are a few important things that you should focus on when it comes to submitting your website to the right search engine. This includes:

- The search engine generator should provide you with automatic updates.
- The registration process should allow you to include the purpose of your business and website.
- Do a quick study to find out where other businesses in your industry are submitting their website.

Your main goal should be to submit your website to as many top search engines as you can so that you get the highest rankings. This will allow your customers and potential customers to find you fast and easily.

Search engine spiders: A search engine spider is a program that methodically travels the Internet looking for all the web pages that have been recently visited and processing this information in a search engine so that pages are indexed and downloaded faster by the user. When you overuse keyword and key phrases you risk this being noticed by search engine spiders and having them bypass your web pages for inclusion into the search engine. Do you want to risk being left out of search engines by being guilty of keyword abuse?

Using a high keyword density may seem like a good idea when you first start developing web content for your website but the hazards far outweigh the risks.

Another mistake that many websites make is choosing their keywords and then not putting these keywords into the any of the relevant content on the web pages. Search engine spiders are programmed to actually need to see the keyword used before it can acknowledge it and index the web page. So why waste time coming up with keywords that don't really have anything to do with what your website is all about only to have search engine spiders overlook your website anyway?

Creating False Web Pages: One of the most serious mistakes that you can make when you're developing the website content for your web pages is to provide your customers with information that has absolutely nothing to do with what you're selling or advertising on your website. Customers who use the Internet to buy a product or service, or simply to find out more information about what you're selling, don't want to arrive at your website pages only to find you're not selling what your offering. If customers are searching for stationary (and you include the keyword "stationary" over and over in your website content to push you up into the high rankings of the search engines) they expect to able to read accurate and dependable information on your web pages about this stationary. If you're not selling or advertising stationary you should avoid using this keyword to pull traffic to your website. Customers who have been tricked will quickly leave your website to find the information that they are looking for elsewhere.

The bottom line is that keyword driven websites don't always work. These websites may get high traffic, and search engine ranking that they want, however customers won't linger to find out what they are really selling. This means a missed opportunity to develop a successful relationship with customers.

Goals for Successful Websites: A quick mention about what your goals should be when you create web pages that are rich with information that customers want to find on the Internet: One of your main tasks when you have an online business is building up your customer database. You want to have as many customers and potential customers on your list as you can so that your online marketing strategy reaches a wide range of consumers.

Once you've built up a customer database you'll want to make sure that you start to gather repeat customers. Repeat sales are the backbone of a successful business and for increased sales. One of the ways that you can achieve repeat sales is by generating great communication with your customers. You can accomplish this good communication by using the following:

- Affiliate programs
- Coupons for repeat customers
- Contests
- Newsletters that provide useful information about what you're selling
- Banner ads
- Discussion groups and forums
- Relationships with associates
- Chatrooms

As mentioned previously you'll already have a lot of customer information that you can use. This includes data that you've collected from previous sales, communication with your customers, and e-mail opt-in lists. You'll also want to collect the information listed here. But just how do you go about gathering that data? There are several different techniques that you can use to get the data that you need to build successful customer databases.

The most important thing to remember is that you always be honest when you're getting information from your customers. If you use deceptive means to get the data you risk losing the trust of your customer. If being honest and above board means that you lose some of those opportunities to capture customer information then realize that the pay off will be the trust and respect you earn from these customers, and potential customers, when they realize that you're doing what you said you would do: asking them to voluntarily to provide you with certain types of information.

The following methods of collecting customer data will help you keep track of sales and profit. This customer data can be found in the following places:

- customer order forms
- warranty card information
- servicing information
- records of returned products
- questionnaires filled out at time of purchase

The above information is very helpful but you'll need a bit more to build up a successful database that includes wide-ranging customer information. This is where some of the newer techniques of data capturing enter the picture. The Internet has provided you with some great opportunities to use technology tools to your advantage. Again, keep in mind that technology is a utensil that you can use and not an end to a means.

All this technology means that you can use some very appealing and winning methods for having your customers leave you the information that you need.

There are many ways that you can correspond with your customers once you've got their interest:

- weekly newsletters
- automated e-mails, targeting one time customers, referrals, and repeat
- customers
- discount or free product offers to customers
- e-mail postcards
- follow up phone calls

Corresponding with your customers is much simpler after you've profiled them and know what they want to see and hear. Database marketing means that you learn as much as you can about your customers and potential customers before sending them any type of messages. Studies show that random messages sent to all your customers often fails since you'll be spending a great deal of time and money to reach only a small portion of those customers that feel you have something to say to them directly.

CHAPTER NINE: BUILDING E-MAIL LISTS

A successful online business requires a trusting relationship with your customers. When your customers know that your online business is reliable and honest they're more likely to buy products or services from you, rather than from your competition. But it's up to you to let your customers know that you're a better choice than your competitor. One way that you can get those important sales is by building up e-mail lists so that you can communicate on a regular basis with your customers.

Never miss an opportunity at communicating with your customers. It's vital to your online company that you come into contact with as many customers and potential customers as possible so that you increase your contacts and eventually increase your sales.

There is so much competition on the Internet and this is why it's important that you stand out for your customers. When your customers know that they can rely on you for dependable service, consistent communication, and quality products or services, they will continue to buy from you time and time again. Your repeat customers will become the mainstay of your business since it's these repeat customers that refer you to their friends and family, thus bringing you more potential customers.

Opt-in Lists: An opt-in list is list of people who have specifically asked to receive more information from your business in the form of e-mail, newsletters, or other types of communication. These people will voluntarily give you their e-mail address to you so that you can communicate with them in the future. Make sure that you build your list of opt-in e-mail addresses so that you can increase the number of customers that you come into contact with.

Online marketing studies show that opt-in e-mailing lists are more successful than other marketing techniques when it comes to sales. When a potential customers requests more information from your business you know that they already have an interest in the product or service that you're selling.

So how do you develop your opt-in e-mailing list? One way that you can start building your e-mail list is by having a place on your website where users can leave their e-mail address.

When you have someone's e-mail address it's up to you to send them an e-mail that is about the products or services that you're selling. Some of the e-mail that you might want to send to your e-mail customers include:

- Newsletters with information about the product or service you're selling, such as information about new products. Newsletters have already been discussed in chapter 5.
- E-zines that have detailed information about what your company sells.
- Discount offers that your send out to only those people on your opt-in list.

The first e-mail that you send out to people on your opt-in list should let them know that they asked to be included on your e-mail list so that they don't think that they are being spammed. As mentioned before, always give people the option to take themselves off your e-mail list at any time. This way they feel that they are in control of all communication with you.

Importance of Building Lists

One of the most important rules of online marketing is the need to have a list of opt-in e-mail addresses. The larger your e-mal list the more successful your online business will be. The bottom line is, if you want to have a successful online business you need to have an opt-in e-mail list.

Many online businesses overlook the other benefits of an opt-in list besides the bottom line of profit. Each time someone buys something from you, you need to make the effort of obtaining their e-mail address. If you don't get your customer's contact information you lose all chance of future communication with them. And this may prevent them from buying from you in the future.

Online marketing studies show that successful online businesses think of their opt-in e-mailing list as their most valuable marketing strategy. Most online businesses keep a back up of their e-mail list so that there is no chance of losing it. Without this e-mail opt-in list your business would lose valuable customer communication which is the backbone of their online success.

The more extensive your e-mail opt-in list is the more advertising you'll generate for your online business. You'll have sales opportunities from your e-mail opt-in list that you wouldn't be able to obtain in any other way. When you regularly stay in touch with your customers you ensure that at least some of them will return to your website for a first purchase or a repeat purchase. E-mail opt-in lists let you communicate with your customers with little or no effort on your part.

Make sure that your online website has opt-in options on every web page. This way people who read your website have every opportunity to give you their e-mail address for future contact with your company.

CHAPTER TEN: FORGETTING ABOUT SEO

Far too many Internet websites rely on content that is based on what is respectively known as "Search Engine Optimization". And just as many of these websites are coming to realized that SEO is not the greatest way to write content for their website customers and potential customers that is going to get them the attention that they want to bring to their online business.

Successful Branding

Successful branding is all about one thing: acknowledgment from your customers. When your customers can recognize your product or service, and detach you from your competition, you've already taken the first step towards grabbing their notice. Branding uses several methods to ensure that your name is out there at the top and that your customers can pick you out from the crowd. Branding has one goal: to gain the confidence of your customers so that they stand by you.

You want to develop branding for your online business that sends a clear meaning in one straightforward package. And you want that brand identification to be an expression of your business and personal style. There are several methods that you can include into your branding strategy to gain recognition for your company.

There are several different techniques of branding that you'll want to consider when you're developing website pages so that they are readable and easily understandable by all your web visitors:

- Visual communication. Create a company logo which is displayed on your packaging and the visual communication you use with your

customers. This includes brochures, business cards, catalogues, stationary letterheads, and other marketing media.
- Creative packaging. Develop packaging for your products that is specific and outstanding to customers.
- beneficial ad campaigns. Take advantage of all media exposure by positively and importantly boosting your public profile.

The approach for successful branding is to keep it simple so that probable customers aren't put off by the audacity of your logo. The strategy for successful branding includes:

- Develop a strong mission statement. Know exactly where your company is going and how you want to get there.
- Define company goals. Be clear on what your business goals are.
- Branding is for your customers. Branding is all about your customers and not about what you sell.
- Dependable marketing tactics. Customers want reliability and simplicity when they identify your product or service.

Branding is all about identification for your company and not just the products or services that you sell.

The end result of successful branding is being able to sell your products or services along with positive recognition from your customers. It's this positive recognition and obligation to your business that develops the strong relationship that you have with your customers and creates profits.

There are many companies both on and off the Internet that use branding successfully so that you can easily recognize them and so that they are a bigger name than their competition. These names have become trusted among consumers throughout the world. With so much business action that is now found on the Internet more online businesses are using branding to have their customers find them and remember them. When it comes to your own online business you need to learn how to use branding in such a way that your service or product stands out among the many Internet websites that are all vying for attention and customers.

Branding is a mixture of inspiration and the type of connection that you're going to have with your customers. The resourceful part of branding is all about the logo (or other branding that you choose to use) and the way that you market on the Internet, and off the Internet, using this logo. The affiliation part of branding is all about the way you make your customer feel when they arrive at your website. You want your customers to feel that they can trust you, and your product or service, so that they generate a sale for your business. The bottom line is that branding offline and online is all about:

- How your product, or service, looks whether it's viewed on your website or on a shelf in your brick and mortar store.
- How your customer feels when they arrive at your website.
- How you deal with customer orders
- The reliability and trust that you earn with your customers using a mixture of branding and successful Internet marketing

Developing your own branding for your business is a key step when it comes to the success of your company. This means that you need to spend value time coming up with the right branding for your products and services.

Market Research

One of the most unbeaten ways that you can find out what customers want to buy, and find out more information about, is to do market studies. When you watch and listen to what it is that customers are interested in, you raise your chances of getting their attention and giving them the information that they are searching for.

Take some time to carefully check the products and the services that you're offering on your website or through your website. You should be asking yourself include (1) what are the rewards and disadvantages to your business of selling or advertising online, (2) will you take payment online, (3) what details will you have to consider about shipping your product to customers, and (4) are you willing to constantly update and keep up your website.

When you have an obvious business idea in mind, and know exactly what it is that you're selling, you'll want to find out what other businesses out there offer the same product or service. You might want to talk to potential customers to see how they react to your product.

Find other websites that are related to your business and take some time checking them out. Look at how they endorse and market similar products or services as well as how each website is laid out and navigated. If a similar website uses a shopping cart for online purchases check it out. See how smoothly the process works and what can be done to perk up the process.

Don't just look at e-commerce sites that are within your own country since customers won't limit their shopping to those countries where they live. Look at the way other countries handle e-commerce websites so that you have a broad spectrum of websites to compare yours with.

Here are some things that you should be asking yourself when you're doing market research for your online business:

- Who are your probable customers?
- What other businesses sell the same products or services?
- Who is going to be your objective market and how are you going to reach them?
- How much will it cost you to market, manufacture, and deliver your product or service?
- Who is your competition?
- How much can you fairly charge for your product or service?

What Are Customers Buying: There are many ways that you can find out what customers are buying both from online businesses and from brick and mortar businesses. Once you find out what customers are buying you can concentrate your website content and articles on what your mainstream customers are looking for. Some of the ways that you can find out what people are buying include:

- Check out the malls. Go to a shopping mall and sit for awhile. Make note of the shopping behaviours of those people who are around you.
- Establish what stores have all the action. Watch to see which stores have the most consumer traffic. Take a look inside to see what is being sold, how it is being sold, how much it is selling for, and how the product is being marketed.
- Take a look at advertising and marketing. Although you may not be selling the same items as those stores in the mall you should still a look at what makes these stores stand out among the rest. How are the products grouped together in the store? How is the product being advertised.
- What you find out from brick and mortar stores can be applied to your online business. Learn what works when it comes to advertising online. Find out what is visually appealing for consumers that makes them want to buy that particular product. .

CHAPTER ELEVEN: WEBSITE DEVELOPMENT

The development of your website design is one of the most central phases of your tactics to establish your position in the market. Without a strong and constructive design you fail to reach the customers necessary for your achievements. The development phase consists of several phases that include:

- Final review of website design.
- Branding
- Development of specific business divisions, such as e-commerce and website.
- Testing
- Taking your website live

There are specific partitions that need to be developed before your web existence and business strategy is ready to go live on the Internet. Once these partitions have been developed your company is ready to reach your customers and secure your position among your competition. Partitions that need to be developed require unique techniques.

Website development: Develop a web presence that is based on your business branding and design. The combination of all three elements will reinforce your online business strength: branding, design, and website development.

E-commerce development: A constructive and easy e-commerce experience is significant for capturing the confidence and self-assurance of your customers. This includes all aspects of e-commerce: product database, product display, security, and shopping cart.

Marketing strategy: The advancement phase is the prelude to your marketing strategy. Marketing requires a strong and solid development phase from which to have a triumphant launch.

The development phase of your business strategy should be as meticulous as possible before you go live with your website. The more safe and sound the multiple divisions of your company existence are the more success you'll maintain.

Your Business Design

Developing a design for your business that augments your image and reinforces your web presence is critical to the success of your business. Your aim is to create a design for your company that you can use across the board: advertising, branding, e-commerce, and web distinction.

The final result of the design procedure is the level transition between all facets of your company exposure to your customers. You want a design that is outstanding and recognizable, and that suggests confidence and reliance from your customers.

There are several strategies that you need to build up in order to accomplish a successful design, design strategy and the design itself. Design strategies include:

- Logo and company identity. Devise a company logo that is introspective of the image you want to portray to your customers.
- Web design. Develop a web design that is revealing, simple to navigate, and impressive to visitors.
- Successful e-commerce. Create an encouraging and easy e-commerce experience for your customers.

Design strategies include:

- Simple Design. Create a design that is uncomplicated and crisp for ease of recognition.
- Bold. Your design should be daring and clear-cut about the statement you want to make yet simple enough to lure customers to

involve themselves in your web pages.
- Interactive. The design of your company should be completely interactive linking the visual communication with your customers and your web presence.

Once you expand your company design you'll soon see a noteworthy return on the investments that you've made, as you reach customers and build up your place among the competition. Design is all about reaching your customers and interacting with them in a way that gets their consideration so they don't forget who you are.

Make sure that you have strategies in place that apply successful and affirmative branding for your business. Some strategies that you should keep in mind include (1) having clear and accurate goals, and know what it is that your company stands for, (2) have a mission announcement that is strong and definite so that you know exactly where your business is going and how you want to get there, (3) be single-minded and unvarying in the way you deal with your customers so that they know what they can expect each time that do business with you, and (4) remember that branding is all about reaching your customers and staying in contact with them. The bottom line is that branding allows you to sell your products or services to customers in a way that makes you stand out from the crowd of competitors that are each looking for their share of Internet business.

Your Internet Image: When you're developing a company representation it means that you'll be creating a "character" for your company that customers can recognize with and want to do business with. The individuality of your company will be a blend of many things, such as the facts of your business, the aims of your business, the style of advertising that you choose to use, and the history of your business. All of these basics will tie together to leave a lasting sense on your customers that can make the difference between the success of your business or its failure. You want to leave a affirmative and lasting impression on the public and your potential customers.

Many large and flourishing companies have worked hard to develop their company image. Part of this illustration is having an image, or brand, that customers can recognize.

Developing your company representation means that you need to identify many parts of your business that include:

- Knowing just who your target market is and how to reach them.

- Developing a company image that is constant and revolves around your target market.

CONCLUSION

Whether you're just starting a new business, or currently have one, it's important that you continue to generate business growth by following five key points. When you focus on the growth of your online business, no matter how successful you already are, you guarantee future profits, further expansion, and continued achievement.

There are some are key points that you need to pay attention to and implement in your business so that you can ensure the further success of your business. These five key points include:

- Build your customer database. Make sure that you use a variety of methods to build your customer database. The more leads that you have the more profits you'll achieve.
- Research your target market. It's important that you have a clear idea of who your target market is. Take the time to research who your competitors are for the products or services that you're selling.
- Deliver what you promise. Don't make false promises to your customers that you can't follow through with. Promising certain products, services, or special deals to lure in people means that you have to follow through with the delivery so that you gain the trust and respect of your customers.
- Have a definite business plan and goals. Make sure that you have a solid business plan so that you know exactly what path you need to take to reach your goals and how long it will take you to get there.
- Advertise and reach your customers. You need to reach your customers so that they can see what products and services you have to offer. Advertising can take place on or off the Internet using newsletters, e-mail automation techniques, or by following leads that are provided by your existing customers.

By including the above five key points in your day to day business practices you'll find that your online business continues to grow in its success.

www.ingramcontent.com/pod-product-compliance
Lightning Source LLC
Chambersburg PA
CBHW050313220526
45465CB00005B/1975